I0430112

Tower Legends

Bertha Palmer Lane

Tower Legends

Bertha Palmer Lane

Table of Contents

I. The Story Told by the Keeper of the Pharos

IN THE year 279 B.C., the Pharos, the great lighthouse, stood on the island of Pharos off the northern coast of Egypt. On a fair morning in that year, Sethos, keeper of the light, and Menna, his sister's boy, were looking down from the top of the tower at the city of Alexandria.

"I want to know how it all began," Menna was saying, "You promised to tell me sometime . . . today?"

"'Tis a big story," answered Sethos deliberately. Sethos was a man of calm movements and steady eyes--Menna's favorite uncle. Menna knew well enough that he could no more be hurried than a sea wave could be hurried to break upon the shore before its time. "But this is the day to tell the story," added Sethos, looking down at the dazzling city of Alexandria, "this is truly the day." "Boy," he exclaimed, with vigor, as he took hold of Menna's arm, "know you today is the greatest day you have ever seen--perhaps ever will see--this day of the festival, of the dedication of the tower?"

Of course Menna knew all that. For, already, at the time of the morning sacrifices, the priests and King Ptolemy Philadelphus had dedicated the newly-finished tower "to the gods, the preservers, for the benefit of mariners," and, in accordance with the king's decree for a day of celebration in honor of his father, Ptolemy, and his mother, Berenice, an immense festival was now in progress. All Alexandria was having a holiday. Everyone was enjoying the varied amusements which were to last from sunrise to sunset. Temples, palaces, gardens were thronged. Chariots, on their way to the race course, were whizzing at breathless speed. Slow-moving elephants, a recent gift to Ptolemy, trod their heavy pace, and behind them stretched a line of camels, with tinkling bells. High-stepping, delicate, Arabian horses, richly caparisoned, had borne their skillful riders in the long procession to the temple of

Isis. Besides Egyptians and Greeks, many foreigners were at the festival--Phoenicians, Libyans, Arabs--all taking part in the gayeties of this first national celebration.

"Know you what a great day this is?" repeated Sethos.

"Yes, I know," said Menna, looking over at the war-fleet brooding like a flock of seabirds on the unruffled water of the Great Harbour. "But I want to hear about the Pharos—*our* Pharos." And he patted the white marble coping as though he loved it. "I can watch the festival go on while you talk."

For Menna had climbed the wide spiral staircase of the lighthouse early this morning on purpose to hear the story he knew his uncle might tell him, if inclined. Like every Alexandrian, he had been watching the Pharos grow higher and higher, year after year. It had been begun in the reign of the present king's father. To Menna, that seemed a long way back, for he himself was only twelve years old. But now, at last, the tall tower was finished. A fortnight ago, his father had taken him out in his boat to show him the immense inscription on the sea side of the tower. It was a Greek inscription in letters of lead, a cubit high and a span wide, that read:

Sostrates of Cnidus, son of Dexiphanes, to the gods, the preservers; for sailors.

There were four main stories of the tower decreasing in size toward the top, and the inscription was at the top of the lowest story. Above it, was a square platform with figures of Tritons. Menna had felt awed when he looked up at the tower. The mighty Pharos! More than four hundred feet it rose into the air and looked fifty miles out to sea. Menna had felt a tingling pride, that day in the boat--pride because he himself had actually seen the majestic tower finished; and, to himself, he said the Pharos should belong to him and he to the Pharos, forever. Sethos, turning from the railing of the lantern platform on which he and Menna stood, said briefly, "I'll tell it, then, boy. There'll never be a better day for it." And as they seated themselves on a low, stone bench, the keeper of the tower, with his eyes constantly on the watch seaward, began his tale.

"This tower really rests upon a huge, glass crab," said Sethos, in a matter-of-fact tone, "and a magician has prophesied that some day a cavalcade of horsemen will lose its way when riding through the three hundred rooms of the colonnaded court from which the tower rises, and will ride into an enormous crack in the crab's back and will be drowned."

Menna looked up quickly at his uncle's face as though to ask a question, but Sethos went on talking in an even tone.

"The lantern beside us, Menna, has to be kept glowing, night and day; at night I have the beacon fire to give reflected light; in the daytime the sun's light is enough. And over our heads is the magic mirror, five spans wide and five spans long, but I am forbidden to reveal to anyone its manner of working. 'Tis made of marvelous and diverse materials. When I sit in a particular place under the mirror, I can see, out there on the ocean, ships invisible to the naked eye. I could see a fleet of enemy ships even a hundred leagues distant. The magician who prophesied about the horsemen has also prophesied that a bold man will some day break into the tower garrison and, while the men are asleep, will come up here and shatter the magic mirror, but," and Sethos spoke positively, "it will not happen in my time." Menna thought best not to ask why, though the lighthouse keeper paused a moment.

"And nothing will ever break the tower itself, boy," went on Sethos. "The marble blocks are strongly cemented together with melted lead. The Pharos is imperishable, even though high waves are constantly breaking against its northern side. This Pharos of ours will outlast everything--a wonder of the world! Eight hundred talents of silver it has cost to build it, and everyone at the festival in Alexandria, today, has helped pay for it, even the Phoenicians and other foreigners. All had to send tax-money. Yes, the Pharos will certainly last forever."

Menna nodded his head wisely.

"The light from this tower seen from afar," said Sethos, "looks like a star. Sailors have mistaken more than once; but they must learn, or the limestone reefs down there will be their ruin." Sethos pointed toward the low-lying northern shore. "Now, Menna," he went on, "if I talk about the Pharos, I must talk about Alexandria. For the Pharos *is* Alexandria, let me tell you, and Alexandria, the Pharos. A long time ago Alexandria didn't exist--only a little village over there; they called it Rhakoti. This was long before the island of Pharos was connected with the mainland by that seven-furlong, stone causeway you took this morning. Rhakoti, the site of present Alexandria, was . . . "

The lighthouse keeper's words were interrupted by a melodious sound coming from one of the statues below on a cornice--a statue that told the hours of the day in loud or soft tones.

"Uncle," said Menna, "does that other statue down below us really shout an alarm if a hostile ship comes in sight?"

"Yes," answered Sethos, "and the outstretched finger of the third statue, there, follows the course of the sun all day long. But about Rhakoti--hear this! When the king had chosen the site for his new city, he assembled workmen and artists and engineers, and ordered great pillars and stones brought from our Egyptian quarries--from lands beyond the sea, too. First, he had the workmen mark, with chalk, some lines on the ground to show the size of the city. When the chalk gave out the workmen used meal, but birds flew down and ate that up! Next, he made a plan for having all the foundations laid at the same moment, when the omens should be favorable. This was what he did. He had a column set before his own tent, with a signal-bell on top. Then along the lines for the city walls he had smaller bells placed, and cords joining them with the large bell, so that, when the signal-bell should ring, the small bells would instantly ring. The king fell asleep, and a bird chanced to light on the cord of the large bell, so, of course, all the little bells rang, too. The workmen immediately obeyed orders and started their work, to the surprise of the king when he awoke!

"Now, after some progress had been made in building the city walls, what happened, think you, boy? They were amazed, one morning, to find no sign of their work--not a stone in place! Watching the next night, they discovered odd-looking beings who came out of the sea and took stones and all else back with them into the water. This troubled the king very much. His shepherd, too--the one called 'a beautiful person'-- who had charge of the king's thousand sheep--was soon in distress. For one day, when his sheep were grazing beside the sea, the shepherd saw a fair damsel come out of the water near him. 'Young man,' the damsel said in a courteous manner, 'I am Lady Marina. Will you wrestle with me for something in return?' 'What would you give?' the shepherd asked. 'If you throw me, I will be yours,' Lady Marina replied; 'if I make you fall, I will have a sheep out of your flock.' 'Content,' the shepherd said. They wrestled and the lady straightway threw him and, taking a sheep, went into the sea. The same thing happened every evening for many weeks, until the king, riding near the shepherd one day, noticed how sad he looked.

"'What is the matter?' asked the king.

"'O King (life, health, and wealth), my lord,' replied the shepherd, 'one of thy sheep is destroyed daily.' Then he told the cause. "After hearing the shepherd's words the king said, 'Take off thy garment.' The man obeyed, and the king, clothing himself in the garment, sat in the shepherd's usual place by the water and told the shepherd to go away.

"When the lady, Marina, came out of the sea, the king wrestled with her and instantly threw her.

"'You are not my former match,' said the damsel. 'To reward you, however, for your victory, I will tell you how to complete the building of your city, for I know you greatly desire this. Know, O King (life, health, and wealth), that the land of Egypt is a land of enchantment. The sea is full of spirits and demons. They are the ones who take away your buildings. To prevent them, follow these instructions. Make large tanks or boxes with transparent sides of glass, and fit covers securely over the top. Put into these tanks men skilled in painting, and put with them meat, drink, and painting equipment. Then fasten the covers down, attach cords from the tanks to ships, and let down the tanks like anchors into the sea. Moreover, be sure that you put little bells on the cords, so that the painters may ring when ready to come up out of the water. Bid the painters paint pictures of the sea-demons that dwell below the waves.'

"The king did all as Lady Marina commanded, and at the end of a week the painters rang the bells and came out of the water bringing the pictures which they had painted. Then Lady Marina said to the painters, 'Make now statues of copper, tin, stone, earth, and wood like your pictures, and set these statues on the shore nearest your building; then when the sea-demons come to demolish the buildings, they will think the statues are opposing spirits ready to fight, and in fear they will return empty-handed to the sea.'

"Everything happened as Lady Marina predicted, for when the sea-demons saw figures exactly like themselves on the shore they fled to the sea and never returned. The building of the city then went on without any hindrance; one marble building after another went up until the whole city of marble shone."

"It's shining today," said Menna, taking a long breath.

"Yes," said Sethos, "it never needs a light, it shines of itself. It's a magnificent city. But there's no more of the tale today, boy; down the spiral staircase you go now, for the next time the statue sounds 'twill be high noon, when you go with your father to see the palace."

Menna pulled himself out of the dream of the past, for

he knew his uncle was to be obeyed. As he stood up, he looked down once more at the brilliant city below the tower. He could see the straight, intersecting lines which were the streets; the undulating line which he knew must be the procession returning to the temple of Serapis; and, nearer the Great Harbour, the fantastic gardens of the Mouseion lying beyond the palace area of Ptolemy. All Alexandria, from the Gate of the Moon at the west, to the Gate of the Sun at the east, shone in a golden light, like a king's crown.

When the boy had gone, the keeper of the tower strolled a few steps back and forth on the platform, and looked toward the Rosetta mouth of the Nile and then toward hazy Lake Mariotis and the mysterious Libyan desert beyond, with its sands of miraculous color. The fingers of the Nile were quietly outstretched toward the waiting sea. Well did the keeper of the tower know all that could be seen from the Pharos, day or night--the expanse of ocean which often seemed a cloud below him; the land of Egypt ever full of mystery; the endless heavens. For a few minutes he stood, silent as the Pharos itself. Then he took his seat directly under the northern edge of the magic mirror, and gazed over the sea.

II. Aeolus and the Tower of the Winds

THE winds of Greece are blowing, today, in sunny Athens, around the Tower of the Winds on Aeolus Street. The tower stands in an enclosed, grassy space, with a few trees and scattered stones--as if left a little aside by the centuries. This tower had its origin in a daydream of Andronicus, lover of winds and stars; for, in spite of the belief of the early Greeks that all dreams live under the earth, Andronicus made his dream live actually on the earth, in plain sight of the Athenians. It was in the first part of the century before Christ that Andronicus was chosen by the people of Athens to plan a tower which should contain a water clock--this new tower to stand not far from the old market-place, on the low land lying north of the Acropolis. Now as Andronicus was something of an astronomer he decided to have sundials, also, on the water clock. So the tower was built, with a turret on the south side to contain the cistern which supplied the water for the water clock. The movement of water wheels caused the gradual rise of a small figure which pointed a rod to the hours on a dial. The Athenians were much pleased with their new water clock, or clepsydra. Greeks of earlier centuries had had to look to the stars for their time at night. "What star is passing?" they would ask. The clepsydra was evidently better than that method; in fact, it was the most important part of the tower! But, to Andronicus, it was of small significance compared with the thought of his beloved winds; for his cherished daydream was that he would represent on the tower all the winds that blow across the land of Greece. Not only that! He would show to passersby in Athens the very wind that was blowing. The people should have their clepsydra, but the tower should have the winds!

Ever since his youthful days in Cyrrhus, Andronicus had cared for the winds and all the tales about them. He had an especially friendly feeling for Aeolus, king of the winds, whose cave, far away in a mountain on the island of Aeolia, north of

Sicily, he knew as well as if he had seen it. Wasn't that cave the home of the winds who were really the sons of Aeolus? Weren't they kept imprisoned there to play merrily or roughly with one another until their royal master at times released one or more of them? Andronicus knew that winds varied as much as men: there were weak winds, strong winds, capricious winds, steadfast winds, winds that did nothing, winds that did everything. When Aeolus sent them forth, in the great bags that mortals call clouds, and bade them carry out his commands, what couldn't they accomplish of joy or sorrow?

Many a tale of Aeolus and the winds, Andronicus had known from boyhood. One of these tales was about Aeolus and Odysseus. In the course of his long voyaging, Odysseus and his comrades came to the island of Aeolia, one portion of which floated continually, yet never floated away. Sur-rounding the steep shore, was a high wall of bronze through which no man could easily break. Behind this protecting wall, Aeolus and his large family dwelt happily, singing and feasting. When the ship of Odysseus neared Aeolia, the gods favored him, for he and his men, by heroic effort, were able to climb the wall of bronze and to enter the island. The heart of King Aeolus instantly warmed at sight of Odysseus, for he gave him welcome to his royal dwelling and bade him and his comrades tarry as long as they would. Joyous feasts now went on, day after day, and, during the feasts, Odysseus, in return for the lavish hospitality of Aeolus, told many a story--stories of Ilium, of the Argive ships, and of the Achaeans. Aeolus and his family listened spellbound. After a month of idleness and feasting, Odysseus became restless for new adventures and told King Aeolus that he was eager to see Ithaca, his home, once more. Aeolus did not try to keep him longer as his guest, and even made him a parting gift. This gift was a huge sack of ox-skin in which all the winds, except the west wind, were tightly bound. When Odysseus boarded his ship, Aeolus himself tied the sack to the mast with a shining silver cord and told the west wind to waft the ship along. Then he bade Odysseus farewell.

Nine days and nine nights, Odysseus and his men sailed on. At dawn, on the tenth day, their hearts were glad because the fields of Ithaca came into view, and, on the shore, men could be seen tending the beacon fires. Odysseus, thankful to be nearing the end of his voyage and utterly worn out by his constant watching, now allowed one of his men to guide the ship, though, during the nine days and nights, he himself had continually held the sheet and carefully watched the course. Sleep immediately overpowered him.

While he slept, his men began to talk among themselves about the sack. One said, "I am sure Odysseus is bringing home gold and silver as gifts from generous Aeolus." Another spoke up angrily, saying, "Why is it all men give high praise to Odysseus, no matter where he goes? Remember you not, when we came from Ilium, he was laden with treasures, but we had nothing? Assuredly King Aeolus has given to him great gifts, but what, now, have we?" And still another bold sailor said, "Come, let us see what is in the sack!" Quickly--for fear Odysseus should wake--they cut down the ox-hide bag.

Instantly, all the winds rushed forth, knocking aside the gentle, west wind, stirring up stormy waves and knocking overboard several sailors. Odysseus, roused by the commotion, awoke in dismay and was inclined at first to throw himself overboard, but then decided to endure his fate, even though he could no longer guide the ship. Covering his head he laid himself down beside his lamenting companions, while the fierce winds drove the ship back to Aeolia. When driven ashore there, Odysseus, taking with him one of his comrades and a herald, climbed again over the wall of bronze and sought the dwelling of Aeolus. Humbly the three sat down on the threshold by the doorposts. Aeolus, his wife and their sons and daughters, looked wonderingly at the suppliants, for some time, before a word was spoken.

"How came you here, Odysseus?" Aeolus then asked. "We sent you forth with all care and help."

"Betrayed was I by my crew," answered Odysseus, "and by treacherous sleep. I pray you help me, for you can." Silence fell upon the hall until Aeolus spoke again. "Out of my island at once!" he shouted. "Know that I will not help twice a man whom the gods have spurned! Begone!"

So Odysseus, lamenting, turned away and sailed on through rough seas, but in his heart he believed the gods were still friendly to him.

Other stories of Aeolus Andronicus could tell, but he preferred the varying winds themselves to the stories of them. Wind lover that he was, he decided, then--when asked to build a tower--to have all the winds seen flying around this tower. For, he said, if all the winds in the world could dwell in one cave, surely the eight chief winds might have a resting-place on a tower, and he would have these eight winds carved in bold relief. He wished--wished, indeed, with all his heart--that Phidias were still alive, to glorify the tower at the foot of the Acropolis as he had glorified the Parthenon on the top. However, Andronicus knew Athenian sculptors who could carve figures of the winds which would be recognizable, at least, and he knew that he himself was able to take a hand in the carving. So the tower was built--a marble tower, eight-sided and on each side, in bas-relief, a flying figure of a wind.

Look, now, at these winds. From the street north of the tower--a street of gay shops to-day--one sees "sky-born" Boreas with his buskins and his thick chiton. As he flies he blows through a shell. Andronicus knew, as did all Greeks, that this Boreas was a powerful fellow, who could come down from hilltops in gigantic strides, uprooting oak trees in his path, or overturning ships. For Boreas was the leader of the strong winds, with wings on his feet as well as on his shoulders, and Homer once said of him, that he, "drove thistle-heads in autumn along the plain."

On the next side of the tower is Kaikias, the northeast wind--an old man, but almost as vigorous as Boreas--carrying in

17

his hand a shield out of which he shakes hailstones, or perhaps ripe olives.

Then comes flying lightly along young Apeliotes, the rainy, east wind, bringing grain and fruit. In the days when the tower was built, Apeliotes looked directly at purple Mount Hymettus that seems to embrace in its wide sweep all Athens. Houses, today, shut out his view of the mountain.

Next to youthful Apeliotes, comes Eurus, the southeast wind--a scowling, bearded man, clad in a long garment, the folds of which he holds rather threateningly before his face. Eurus brings storms. His warm breath melts snow, but makes rain fall. From his wings, declared the Greeks, a heavy mist falls upon the slopes of the hills and a blinding fog creeps over the sea. No wonder sailors despaired when Eurus blew!

Facing the Acropolis is Notus, the showery south wind-- a youth lightly clothed and barefooted, who holds an inverted jar from which rain may pour. Notus was sometimes a favoring wind, but often, an adverse one. Andronicus could have told you of the time when Notus, in company with Eurus, Zephyrus, and Boreas, "forth rushed together" to overwhelm Odysseus, at Poseidon's command to the waves to raise a storm. Another time, Odysseus safely passed the rocks of Scylla and Charybdis and moored his ship for many days in a safe harbor, and "all that month incessant south winds blew."

Barefooted Lips flies next to Notus. He carries the aplustre, the stern ornament of a ship, to show that he wafts the ships home in safety. All Greek sailors love Lips, the southwest wind.

On the west side of the tower, which faces the old market-place with its stately entrance-gate, floats airily along; Zephyrus, the west wind. He is a young man and, as he flies, he scatters flowers from the folds of his garment. Zephyrus, both gentle and "hard-blowing," once aided the voyage of Telemachus, son of Odysseus, when the goddess Athene sent "a

18

brisk, west wind that sang along the wine-dark sea"; but after Odysseus, in his journeyings, had left the Island of the Sun "a shrill west wind arose blowing a heavy gale."

Between Zephyrus and Boreas, the northwest wind is flying, Skiron, who dries up the earth with a scorching blast. He is an old man, carrying a brazier of hot charcoal.

These, then, are the winds of Aeolus, summoned by Andronicus to dwell on the tower. Day and night, the winged figures fly around the tower. To show which wind, at any moment, was strongest, Andronicus surmounted the top with a bronze Triton, turned by the breeze, his rod pointing downward at the figure of the particular wind then blowing. The Triton perished long ago, as did also the two porticoes of the tower. But, under each figure of a wind, are still the lines of a sundial, with a projecting bar of metal, from which Athenians, even today, can tell the hour, if they wish.

Three divinities guarded the tower: Apollo, the sun-god, without whose power mortals could not have known the true sun time; Poseidon, god of the sea, in whose charge was the water that supplied the clepsydra; and Aeolus, who held the mastery of the winds. Moreover, Athene, eternal wisdom, is perpetual guardian, for an inscription on a piece of architrave dedicates to her the whole tower.

For twenty centuries, the winds of Greece have swept around this small, plain tower--tempestuous, uncertain winds of winter, or gentle, persistent winds of summer. For twenty centuries, the sun has told the time upon the dials of the tower. Andronicus did not think it necessary to build a tower as high as Olympus to win the protection of the gods, nor one as high as the clouds to secure the presence of the winds. For he was sure that the mighty winds who once dwelt in a cavern would be content, also, in keeping close to even a low tower of their own. Ages before the tower was built, Aeolus had bidden his winds leave their cave in Aeolia and fare forth through the world. So Boreas, Zephyrus, and the rest, departing from Aeolia, had blown across Italy, and across Greece to the Delphi Mountains, and beyond. The same winds are blowing, today, in Athens, around the Tower of the Winds, on Aeolus Street.

III. The Moon That Shone on the Porcelain Pagoda

THE mid-autumn moon was shining on the high pagoda that stood outside the Red Bird Gate, the southern entrance to Chin-ling, China. Wing Ling (Peaceful Forest), a wide-awake boy, had just this moment remarked that he hoped the moon would shine bright enough to drop down money for heaps of moon-cakes. He and his brother, Li Sun (Pear-tree, Son-of-Li), were sitting on the lowest of the four wide steps leading to the broad, octagonal base of the Porcelain Pagoda. "Liu li t'a" was its real name, that is, Vitreous-substance-of-liquid-gems-pagoda. Early in the fifteenth century, the emperor, Yung-lo (Eternal Joy), had the pagoda erected as a token of gratitude to his mother, the Heart-of-kindness-showing, Ever-gracious Empress. The people of Chin-ling sometimes called it "The Temple of Gratitude," but to Wing Ling and Li Sun it was always the Porcelain Pagoda, because of the colored slabs of glazed porcelain--green, yellow, and red--which covered the brick-work.

Wing Ling and his brother had often seen the pagoda in the daytime when it looked gay and airy, especially when glittering sunshine fell upon the painted balconies, the delicately carved balustrades and porcelain slabs. Only once a year, were the boys allowed to see it at night--the night of the moon-festival. When the mid-autumn moon was biggest and roundest, a festival, all the moon's own, was celebrated by everyone, and, on this night of nights, Chinese children had the fun of eating delectable moon-cakes *if* the moon showered down money enough to buy the cakes. Li Sun said now that he noticed the moon was shining brighter than usual and probably the brightness would make a bigger moon-shower! The two boys, seated on the pagoda step, were easily unobserved, for men, women, and children in holiday dress were coming and going in such throngs that no one paid any attention to them. The moon--

21

the splendid, round moon with the rabbit at its lower edge--was the only important thing tonight.

Moonlight and lantern light were vying with each other in illuminating the Porcelain Pagoda. By moonlight, the slender, octagonal building, mounting story by story far toward the sky, looked mysterious, fantastic, unreal. As if moonlight were not enough, a hundred and forty lights were gleaming from top to bottom of the pagoda. The seventy-two windows, eight in each story, were now ablaze with lantern light. As if gayety and mystery and lights were not enough, two hundred little bells, some of brass, some of porcelain, were softly tinkling in the slight breeze. For, from the golden ball and pine-apple that crowned the metal spire, chains of bells hung down to the angles of the highest roof, and more bells hung from all the corners and edges of the nine roofs. Tonight, the melody of the bells was like the melody the Great River--the Yangtze River-- makes at its source where it flows, in rippling beauty, over golden sands.

"Li Sun," abruptly said Wing Ling, "do you know this Porcelain Pagoda never throws any shadow toward the west? The priests say so, and they must know, because they have charge of the pagoda and they protect all the images of the idols and saints--two thousand of them--here in the pagoda. And the priests know all about . . ."

"*I* know it's time for the moon-cakes to be eaten," interrupted Li Sun.

"I'll tell the moon-tale first," said Wing Ling, "or perhaps there'll not be any moon-cakes." Yet, as he spoke, the rascal knew that luscious moon-cakes were, this minute, in the large, inner pocket of his sleeveless jacket, and in Li Sun's pocket, too. Moon-cakes with glistening, round, sticky places on them! Moon-cakes that had on them little, sugar rabbits! Moon-cakes that had a bulging sugar toad! No wonder Li Sun thought it time to eat the moon-cakes! No wonder Wing Ling felt happy at the mere thought of them!

22

"Tell the tale, then," said Li Sun, cheerfully laying aside his great hunger, because he knew that his older brother who liked so much to talk wouldn't eat till the story was told.

"Here it is," began Wing Ling, as he and Li Sun wriggled themselves back into the corner of the step to be out of the way of people's feet. "Once the Emperor, Ming Wong, was walking in the moonlight--moonlight just like this; and he was on a terrace . . . "

"The Feng Huang terrace? Where the three phoenix birds sang, one springtime, so wonderfully all the other birds came to listen?" asked Li Sun eagerly.

"I forget. Perhaps it was that terrace--perhaps another. He was walking up and down, and his courtiers were with him . . ."

"How many courtiers?" broke in Li Sun.

"Interrupt me not, O Small-Devil," said Wing Ling, "or I stop telling the tale. The Emperor, with his flute in his hand, was walking up and down, when he asked one of his courtiers this question, 'Of what is the moon made, Noble-Servant?'

"The courtier said to the courtier standing nearest him, 'His Highness, the Emperor, asks of what the moon is made.'

"The second courtier quickly turned to another courtier, saying, 'His Highness, the Emperor, asks of what the moon is made.' The third courtier asked a fourth courtier; the fourth asked a fifth; the fifth, a sixth; the sixth, a seventh; and the seventh courtier ran as fast as the men ran who were sent by the Great Ch'in to find the dragon. I tell you, Li Sun, they ran fast! The seventh courtier ran, like the red fire, to catch up with a magician walking toward the city wall, and he did catch up with him, and seized the magician's garment. Out of breath he was, after that run, but he panted these words, 'The Emperor, His Royal Highness . . . would know . . . of what . . . the moon is made.' Without a word, the magician turned at once and ran back all the way to the terrace where the Emperor was still

23

walking, still looking at the moon. Prostrating himself on the ground before the Emperor's feet, the magician said, 'Would His Highness, the Emperor, like to visit the moon and see of what it is made?'

'Let it be so!' replied the Emperor.

"The magician instantly threw his staff into the air toward the moon, and, lo, a rainbow bridge from earth to moon! As soon as the Emperor and the magician had stepped upon the bridge it rose beyond reach of the astonished courtiers and became like a wisp of cloud.

"The Emperor and his guide walked as easily as anything right along the rainbow bridge toward the moon, and I tell you, Li Sun, the moon shone amazingly bright, the nearer they went. When they stepped from the bridge to the surface of the moon, the Emperor noticed that most of the golden shining came from the thick groves of cassia trees--yes, Li Sun, the moonlight came straight from the cassia trees which were in full flowering. At the foot of a tall cassia, near the end of the bridge, crouched a little, white jade hare.

'Who is he?' asked the Emperor.

'That is He-who-pounds-drugs-for-the-Genii,' answered the magician. 'He uses the cinnamon bark for the drugs. On clear nights in mid-autumn you can see him from the earth.'

"The Emperor and the magician then walked along the broad avenues of the pale yellow cassia trees and saw, on either side, radiant palaces, sparkling towers and twinkling streams. Fair ladies, in rainbow-colored robes, came out to meet them, and, after bowing and smiling and saying welcoming words, passed on their way. Strange flowers, that looked far away though they were near at hand, covered the fields with silver-white or golden bloom. Snowy-white birds, with eyes like stars, flew in and out the golden cassia branches. Ah, it was a great glory, there, on the moon, Li Sun! And it's the same moon that shines down here tonight on this pagoda. But there's more to the

24

story."

"Tell it," said Li Sun, sleepily.

"The magician said to the Emperor," went on Wing Ling, 'Do you see that frog?'

'Yes,' said the Emperor.

"Then the magician told him this story: Once the Pearl-of-Heaven, the Moon, was about to be swallowed by a dragon, when an Archer Lord shot arrows into the sky, and so saved the moon from destruction. The Archer Lord was rewarded by a gift of a pill which would make him live forever. But, afterwards, his wife stole the magic pill and fled to the moon. That didn't help her any, for, as soon as she stepped upon the - grass of the moon, she was turned into a frog. Here in the moon she still lives. Are you awake, Li Sun?" suddenly asked Wing Ling.

"By the Moon-Toad, Heng-O, I *am*! Go on!" answered Li Sun, briskly.

"Hear now the ending," said Wing Ling. "When the Emperor and the magician left the moon and were coming down the rainbow bridge, the Emperor spoke not a single word, but he played on his flute. As he played, lovely strains fell to earth. Then he took coins, from the pouch on his girdle, and threw them from the bridge, and the money dropped at the feet of children. Wasn't that fine, Li Sun?--Don't you wish . . .?"

But just then a man and a woman, dressed in brightest of embroidered silk robes, bent over the two boys, who jumped to their feet as the man's words carne like a swift stream pelting down a steep mountainside.

"O wicked boy, Wing Ling!" exclaimed the man. "O abominable urchin, Li Sun! Why, oh, why, have you been hiding from your honorable parents all this long time? What have you been doing? Where have you been? We have walked hour after hour searching for you. We have called on metal, wood, water, fire, earth. We have earnestly petitioned them all to direct us to the greatly-desired-place-of-hiding of our disobedient and much-to-be-despised sons. We have begged them, implored them, to lead us to that hiding-place wherever it might be--whether on the bank of the Great River or in some spot in our pride-of-the-heart city of Chin-ling, our wide city that lies between the dragon's paws. 'Tis well I propitiated the deities by my worthy contribution toward the expense of the wonder-of-darkness lights on this pagoda. For, as the streams of light, from the cassia branches in the moon, fell upon this lantern-lighted pagoda--this Vitreous-substance-of-liquid-gems-pagoda--and as we saw the pagoda lights that illumine the thirty-three heavens, that detect the good and evil among men, that ward off human miseries, we quickened our steps hither, and lo, in this Temple-of-Gratitude pagoda, here we find you! We find you at last--our always-cherished, always-beloved sons!"

The father paused, breathless; and the mother said to the boys quietly, "Sons, have you eaten your moon-cakes yet?"

Late in the evening, the moon still shone down upon the city of Chin-ling. The light from the waving branches of the cassia trees in the moon streamed upon the Porcelain Pagoda, while the bells of the tower tinkled in the breeze from the Heaven-High Mountains. The moonlight shone, also, on the silent avenue, bordered with statues, outside the T'ai'ping Gate. It shone on the wall that meandered for miles around Chin-ling, and on the throngs of people strolling homeward through the Red Bird Gate; and it shone on the home of Wing Ling (Peaceful Forest) and Li Sun (Pear-tree, Son of Li).

As the boys were going to bed, the little jade hare looked down at the glistening earth. Li Sun, looking up at the moon, said to his brother, "Wing Ling, I can see the white-jade hare tonight--I see him pounding the moon-drugs!"

IV. The Brahman's Star

A Tale of Kutb Minar

LATE one afternoon, a few centuries ago, a Brahman, who was toiling along the hot plain south of Delhi in North India, kept his eyes fixed upon the distant tower of Kutb Minar. This solitary tower was the only break in the wide stretch before him. Occasionally, the Brahman stopped to rest, leaning on his staff, but, even then, his eyes hardly glanced away from Kutb Minar.

"Nearer," once he muttered aloud; "nearer! I'll make it yet!" On he went, mile after mile, over the hot ground, leaving, far behind him, the magnificence of Delhi, where he had allowed himself to rest a very little while in the course of his long journey on foot from the north. He had the air of one making a pilgrimage--of an iron-willed man who would let nothing come between him and his goal. No wind should check his gait, nor burning sun delay him. Never did soldier, merchant, or slave go on more steadily whether driven by his own will or by another's. One clear thought was in the Brahman's mind--that if he didn't stop, he would reach Kutb Minar before nightfall. As he trudged along, he nodded complacently at the thought. Yes, this steady pace would certainly bring him to the tower before dark.

Now Kutb Minar was a good eleven miles from Delhi, and the Brahman was no longer young, but the growing nearness of the tower had added strength to him each hour, especially during the last mile. For some time, his eyes had been gladdened by the nearer view of the domes and minarets of the stately mosque, beside which the tower rose. At length, he began to see more clearly the tower itself, as it stood gleaming in the sunset light, a tapering shaft of sunset glory. For the modulated shades of sandstone--purplish red at the base, pink in

27

the second story, dark orange at the summit--glowed in the yellow radiance of the setting sun with such dazzling reflection that anyone less wise than a Brahman would have found it hard to tell which light was of earth and which of the sky. The two upper stories, glistening with white marble, appeared to his eyes like the portal of heaven, concealing the mystery of all Hindu thought.

As the Brahman, absorbed in his meditations, slowly walked along, a tiger, limping, approached him. When the Brahman was aware of the tiger he stopped, not through fear, but sympathy.

"You have hurt your paw," he said, kindly.

"Sir," said the tiger deferentially, "if your heart prompts you to help me I will repay you at some future time in any way that I can."

"No payment do I want," replied the Brahman. "Let me see your paw!"

The tiger, sitting on his haunches, lifted his right forepaw from which a splinter of wood protruded. With deft fingers the Brahman extracted the bit, and, before the tiger could utter his thanks, said, smiling, "If *your* heart prompts you to help me and all mankind, see that the rest of your days and nights you make not too free use of that great strength given in the beginning to your ancestors and thereby to you. Remember you owe your life to man's kindness, because man's skill is ahead of all your strength. I must now go on my way."

"Sir," said the tiger, "I owe you great thanks, and I will remember." With that, he bounded away across the plain.

The Brahman plodded on with quicker steps to make up for the interruption. "Before the sun reaches that low cloud," he said to himself, "I shall be at the tower." And before the sun entered the cloud he was by the base of the tower. Standing near it for some moments, with bowed head and folded arms, he might have been a statue--a statue with turban and robe that

28

seemed a part of the sunset light.

Then he looked up with interest at the picturesque Arabic characters cut in the five dark bands around the lower stories. In the lowest band he saw five separate divisions of hieroglyphics, giving the titles of *Kutab-ad-din* --the first of the shepherd kings of Delhi--and Kutab's proclamation of himself as Sultan of all India; also, the name of Kutab's master, Muhammed Ghori, with words in praise of him. There were verses from the Koran, and an invocation to Visna Karma, "the celestial architect of the Hindus." Part of the higher inscription, too, the Brahman read:--"Kutb Minar commenced in 1200 by the Amir, the Commander of the Army . . . of the Sultan Muhammed Ghori, to celebrate the great victory."

As the rest of the inscription was becoming hard to make out in the lessening light, the Brahman walked around to the door of the tower. Within the doorway sat a man weaving a small tapestry.

"Good-evening to you, O guardian of the Tower of Victory!" said the Brahman, pleasantly.

The doorkeeper, on seeing the Brahman, rose immediately with a word of greeting and added, "Sir, you arrive late in the day!"

"Day and night are one for me," answered the Brahman. "Have you many travelers, nowadays, to see the tower?"

"But few," said the doorkeeper. "You, sir, are the first for six days."

"A lonely life for you," remarked the Brahman. "No, sir," replied the man, quietly. "I have the sky both day and night."

The Brahman gave a keen glance at the doorkeeper's calm face, but made no comment. Taking a coin from his belt, he put it into the man's hand, and, with a look toward the west where the flaming sun was just now dropping below the

29

horizon, he entered the doorway.

"I shall spend the night on the tower," he said, as he began to climb the stairs.

"A good night be yours, sir!" answered the guardian of the tower.

For a man no longer in his prime, the stairs were very many. Three hundred and seventy-eight steps at the end of an eleven mile walk from Delhi! Was the Brahman mad that he thought he could climb them? Old or young, mad or sane, up he climbed, stopping whenever his breath gave out, and improving those wasted moments by uttering prayers. Many a prayer there had to be during his climb, for, in truth, he went up more and more slowly. Not even a view from the tower did he have, for two excellent reasons: the stairway was dark, and he climbed with his eyes closed, just as the Indian saint of old climbed the mountain. Up, up, up,--steps, pauses, prayers; up, up, up,--more rests, more prayers, more steps, until, finally, the top!

Breathing heavily after his climb, the Brahman stepped out upon the narrow platform at the fifth story and looked westward. The brilliant clearness of the sky had already become dull and metallic-looking, except for a single, quivering star. He looked toward the northeast, in the direction of the lofty Himalayas, the overwhelming mountains that belonged, he knew, to the sky-dwellers--their snow-covered tops always as billowy as ocean wave-crests. Presently he became absorbed in the majestic scene before him; the river Jamna, flowing slowly near Delhi, saffron in the twilight; the tomb of the ancient sultan, Altamsh, now a dark spot on the sand; the iron pillar-- that old East Indies pillar--in the courtyard of the mosque. At a distance, he could make out the shadowy, blurred clumps of pomegranate and banyan trees, and could barely see the outlines of the temples of Delhi. Far beyond, he knew the mighty Ganges was forging along, ever protected by those sky-dwelling mountains. With folded arms he stood quietly for a long time, watching the light in the sky turn from copper color to deep bluish gray, until stars filled all space. Plain, rivers, mountain-tops vanished, but stars were overhead and all around--multitudes of stars. The Brahman, with a whimsical smile, suddenly looked directly up to the very bright star over his head, and began talking softly.

"Mother Star," he said, in a happy voice, "I've come back. You know why. You know how my father brought me to the top of this tower when I was a boy, and told me your story. Mother Star, once, when you were sick, your two sons, the Sun and the Wind, and your daughter, the Moon, went to a feast. You lay on your couch, hour after hour. The elder son came home first. 'What have you brought me, Son?' you asked. 'Nothing, Mother,' answered the Sun; 'don't you suppose I wanted the good time for myself?'

"Soon the second son came in. 'Have you brought home anything for me, Son?' you asked. 'Nothing whatever, Mother,' the Wind replied; 'the feast was for the young.'

"Then the daughter came singing down a shaft of light. 'See, Mother,' she called out gaily, before you could speak; 'see what I have brought you--fruits and sweet cakes!'

"She made you glad, Mother Star; the Moon-daughter made you glad. And as my father finished telling me the old tale he said to me, 'Son, you are a descendant of Mother Star, even as the king of Delhi was a descendant of the moon. When you are no longer young, come back to this tower if you have brought from the feast of life any blessings for others.'

"Mother Star, I am here. No one but you may ever know."

Taking, from an inner pouch, a pomegranate and a sweet cake, the Brahman laid them on the highest bit of ledge he could reach. Then he raised his hands toward the luminous star overhead. Presently, he let his hands drop, folded, upon his breast, and he stood almost as motionless as the star itself.

After a while, he sat down on the stone platform, and

31

was lost in thought. He thought of King Bharata, that famous, early king of Delhi, who was descended from the moon; he thought of the tale of the Ganges--how the river had been brought, as a maiden, to earth and had never regretted leaving her heavenly home. As he glanced in the direction of the Khyber Pass, he recalled the hordes of invaders who had come like strong winds into the land of India--Greeks, Persians, Afghans, Tartars, savage chieftains--always pushing on and on, while the stars, then as now, were serenely shining over the plain. Most of all, he thought of Mother Star, because the vivid remembrance of that night on the tower long ago, and the clear vision of the star, had possessed him throughout his long life. He had been a traveler in many lands and was a learned man besides. Many languages he knew, and under-stood the arts, astronomy, medicine, the winds that swept the ocean, and the talk of all animals and birds. Year after year, men in cities, and animals in the jungle, had sought his counsel. His life had been spent largely out of doors, so that he deeply revered the sun and the lightning, the mountains and the winds, and, especially, the cloudless sky and its presiding god, Indra. Yet, in his heart, from boyhood to manhood, he had always seen the star as he had seen it when his father told him the tale. Nothing on earth or in the sky had ever held for him such beauty, such reality, such inspiration, as Mother Star. To Mother Star he owed all that he was himself and all that he had brought to others. His offering, to-night, then, was more, far more, than a pomegranate and a sweet cake--it contained the blessings for others which he had brought from the feast of life.

At dawn, an old Brahman was making his slow way across the plain toward Delhi. Behind him, the tower of Kutb Minar, catching the first rays of the sun, shone like a rainbow flame.

Suddenly a tiger bounded toward the Brahman and on reaching him said, "Sir, I owe you great thanks, and I have remembered all night." Then, together, the Brahman and the tiger walked toward the sunrise, talking agreeably as they went.

32

V. The Dragon of Ghent

AT ONE side of the Place Saint Bavon in the center of Ghent, Belgium, rises the impressive carillon tower with its fifty-two singing bells. On the largest bell, which is taller than a tall man, is a Flemish inscription that reads:

"My name is Roland. When I toll there is fire. When I ring there is victory in the land."

This great bell might vie with the horn carried by that other Roland, the knightly champion of Charlemagne--a horn that was heard twenty miles. On top of the belfry, is a weather vane, of dragon shape, that presides over all the winds, hot or cold, and rejoices when Roland rings.

A long, long, time ago, before the dragon began to live on the tower, he lived near Aleppo, one of the chief cities of the Saracens in northern Syria. He was such a tender-hearted old dragon that he was called The Weeping Dragon, because he wept large bucketfuls of tears whenever the Belgian crusaders and the Saracens fell to fighting. Now, as the Saracens and Belgians fought at the slightest provocation, the tears of the sympathetic dragon flowed with such abundance into the ground that the soil became unusually fertile, and there soon grew up, from this rich soil, a rare flower. The Belgian crusaders, delighted with the bright-colored flower, called it The Turk's Turban, though it is a pity they didn't know The Weeping Dragon well enough to name it for him. Buccoleon was the dragon's name. When the last Saracen war was over, one of the crusaders, Taff, a lover of flowers, brought back the seeds of The Turk's Turban to Flanders and planted them in his own garden. Beautiful tulips rewarded him, tulips of brilliant color, that brought him high praise and much money, too.

The fame of these tulips spread far, until it reached even Buccoleon himself, who, now that the wars had ceased, had

33

been living in his quiet marshes in the outskirts of Aleppo. A soothsayer, ages past, had predicted that, if the Saracens and Belgians should ever stop fighting, the tears of The Weeping Dragon would dry up and his brown scales would turn to scales of pure gold. So it proved. For, when all the wars had come to an end, the dragon no longer felt like weeping, and his sombre, brown scales were gradually replaced by gleaming scales of gold.

Now, one afternoon, as Buccoleon lay luxuriously in the sunny marsh, he had a thought, as new and glittering as his scales--he would fly to Flanders to see the tulips which rumor said he himself had given to the earth. Since he had only a vague notion of the whereabouts of Flanders and Ghent, he decided to ask advice of a marsh bird hovering near him.

"Tell me," said Buccoleon, "you birds fly everywhere and hear everything--how shall I go to the garden of Taff?"

"Easily told," whistled the bird. "My brother was there last month. Fly northward, and then northwest, until you see the Bosporus, the Golden Horn and the Marmora. After you arrive at stately Constantinople, ask the clouds that float at daybreak over the citadel and they will tell you more."

"Thanks," said the dragon, "I'll start at once."

So he wriggled from jaw to tip of tail, complacently glanced along his own shining ridges, reared up with a convulsive tremor that woke all Aleppo babies from their naps, and, with a great bound, shot into the air. Aleppo had never experienced such a surprise. The men of Aleppo, dazed, looked first at the dragon soaring aloft and then at one another and exclaimed, "What! . . . the dragon? . . . the dragon going away?" The boys of Aleppo all pointed up to the sky and cried out, "The dragon! The dragon! . . . Let's follow him! . . . Come on! Let's follow Buccoleon!" And they ran down the road. The women stood in their doorways wringing their hands and said, "The dragon gone! . . . What *shall* we do without our dragon? . . .

34

We've always had our dragon."

But presently all realized that to try to keep the dragon was useless. For dragons--at least good dragons like Buccoleon-- always get what they want, and Buccoleon wanted to go away. So all the people--men, women, and children--stood watching the great dragon soar off toward the northwest until he was only a speck in the blue distance and, finally, not even a speck. Then they went back to their daily tasks in Aleppo, and found, rather to their astonishment, that life was much the same, even without the dragon.

Meanwhile, Buccoleon was well started on his adventure. Far from Aleppo he flew and flew until, one early dawn, he reached a large city.

"Is this Constantinople?" inquired Buccoleon of a pink cloud.

"It is," the cloud replied.

"Tell me, please," went on Buccoleon, "how shall I go to the garden of Taff? Clouds, like you, see every place under the sky."

"Yes, we do," agreed the cloud. "I can tell you how to go. Aim northwest to Vienna, then ask the Danube River to tell you the way."

Swiftly the dragon flew and flew, until he came to the broad Danube at Vienna, and good it seemed to Buccoleon to rest beside water again.

"Tell me, River," he said, "how shall I go to the garden of Taff? A river like you wanders far and must know all that's worth knowing."

"That is true," murmured the Danube clearly. "I can tell you the best way to go to Ghent. Steer a little to the west of north and fly onward till you see the towers and turrets of Nuremburg castle. Then ask the wind to show you the rest of your course."

The dragon left the Danube, somewhat reluctantly, and whiffled along all night under the stars toward old Nuremburg. In the morning, he poised himself over the castle turrets where a strong wind was blowing.

"Wind," shouted Buccoleon, "how shall I go to the garden of Taff? Winds blow everywhere and see everything."

"Come along with me," called back the wind; "I'm going there myself, as it happens, this very morning."

Now, as the dragon and the wind journeyed together, the dragon said, "Have you ever chanced to see the garden of Taff?"

"Many times," answered the wind. "How does it look?" asked Buccoleon.

"Like a sunset spread over the ground," said the wind.

"Are the tulips of one color?" inquired Buccoleon.

"Of as many colors as the rainbow," replied the wind; "some are like palest moonlight, others are like deep tree-shadows; and when I let one of my breezes stir them, gently, the flowers are like dancing flames."

"Ah," said Buccoleon, "that's what I want to see."

Not long after this talk, the wind pointed downward. "Look!" he said, "do you see a gleam of color over there?"

"I do," answered Buccoleon with a jubilant ring in his voice. "It is fairer than anything I have ever seen." But, just as he spoke, an arrow smote him, and he fell headlong to the earth . . . .

The dragon's fall looked like the fall of a glorious golden star. People, for miles around, rushed toward the bell tower. The first to reach the tower was a tall, resolute man, liked by everybody.

"Now who sent that wicked arrow?" he cried.

A boy in the crowd made answer. "Archers went up into

the high watchtowers yonder, this morning."

"Archers?" exclaimed the man. "Who sent them there?"

Then Taff, the florist, and his friend Nyken, the potter, made their way through the throng until they were beside the tall man. "Mynheer," said Taff, "the goldsmiths have been envious of me because my tulips have done so well and have brought fortune my way. Perchance they sought to kill the dragon for his golden scales, to make themselves richer."

And the potter, Nyken, nodded his head, saying, "Aye, they said as much to the baker yesterday."

Other friends of Taff now told the story of The Weeping Dragon of Aleppo whose tears had caused the marvelous tulips to grow. Then, with one accord, it was voted that Buccoleon should receive the utmost honor and should have his place on the pivot of the iron weather vane on top of the belfry. The tall leader suddenly raised his right arm and pointed up to the bell tower, as he shouted, "Victory!--not death for the dragon, but victory! He shall live among us forever!"

All the people took up the word, crying, "Victory!" while the leader, and Taff, and Nyken entered the tower and climbed up the stairs to the bells.

Soon came the voice of Roland ringing a mighty tone of gladness, and proclaiming far and wide the words so well known:

"When I ring, there is victory in the land."

There on the bell tower, today, is the golden dragon--a shining figure--turning, turning with the winds, morning, noon, and night, and looking down at the gardens of tulips in Ghent.

VI. The Ox That Helped

A Legend of Laon

GRAND-PÈRE Jean sat on a low bench outside the doorway of his little cottage on the Laon hillside. As far as his old eyes could see were sunny vineyards with giant trees beyond--trees that had been part of the forest of St. Gobain when Charlemagne was crowned king of the Franks. Wherever the old man looked were fields gay with poppies, and a landscape that smiled. Little François, bare-kneed, and clad in black apron, looked up from his marbles on the ground and said, suddenly, in his direct way, "Grand-père, you will tell me about the ox that helped?" And he looked toward the Cathedral.

From the doorway of the cottage, they saw the towers of the Cathedral--the two, octagonal belfries, with the huge oxen and horses guarding the summits. From lofty stalls, the animals gazed over the V-shaped valley that was now filled with the clear, abundant sunlight of early afternoon. Grand-père Jean's quiet hands rested on his cane as he tranquilly gazed at the Cathedral towers which were so still, so still, against the sky. The boy aimed one more marble at its enemy marble, then leaned back against the wall of the cottage.

"Grand-père," repeated François, with a tiny show of authority, "You will begin the story? . . . You know the one-- about the ox that helped?"

"But yes," assented the grandfather, without moving his peaceful hands, "the ox that helped! Listen well, now, my François! It was years and years ago . . ."

"Last time you told it you said it was before you were born," interrupted François.

"But yes, my child, before I was born, that is true; years ago, it was, centuries ago. Count back, François, count back

38

with me--twenty, nineteen, eighteen, seventeen, sixteen, fifteen, fourteen, thirteen . . . the thirteenth century it was--about seven hundred years ago, when the men of Laon were building up, again, the great church. Our France had been having a hard time. Our Laon had been having a hard time. This town had had to fight for its liberties. It had had to fight against the invaders, and this, too, though Laon was one of the three great fortresses. For know this, François--La Fère, and Reims, and Laon--these are the fortresses--the fortresses then and the fortresses now."

"The fortresses I know all about," said François, as he made a triangle with three marbles. "Here they are."

"Now, François," went on his grandfather, "I tell you it was no easy thing the men of Laon had to do after our great church had been burned by the invaders. They had to build the church anew. They had to carry the great stones from the ancient quarries in the low valley down there,"--and Grand-père Jean pointed down the hillside. "They had to carry the great stones, from the plain, up the steep hill, every day, so long as stones were needed to build up this church of ours. And, I tell you, my François, when young Enguerrand fought with the lion that lived in the woods between Laon and Soissons, he had no harder task; for it was only once that Enguerrand fought--he fought the lion just once, and killed him. But these men, these sturdy men, worked day after day with all their strength, for months and months. They found the work hard, hard."

"And the oxen?" put in François.

"But yes, the oxen were the biggest helpers of all," continued Grand-père Jean. "They and the horses dragged the carts laden with the stones or with the heavy wood, but the oxen were stronger than the horses. All day long, from morning till night, the patient oxen toiled up the steep hill slowly, slowly, with their loads. And, François, let me tell you, they *wanted* to draw the loads. Yes, they climbed the hill eagerly, every time. You could tell by looking at them how glad they were to help. They never had to be urged."

"You didn't see them, Grand-père," said François firmly, though in a half-questioning tone.

"No, François," said Grand-père Jean, "I didn't see them, but I know how they looked."

"I, too," agreed François.

"Now it happened that the sun was very hot one day," went on his grandfather, "hotter than usual; and four oxen, dragging up a heavy load of stones, suddenly stopped. My faith, but one of those oxen was tired out! Too tired the poor beast was to take another step! The good driver, Pierre, unhitched the ox from the cart to let him rest at the side of the road. As the tired animal lay down on the grass, his beautiful, large eyes looked up at his kind master gratefully.

"'*Pauvre bête! Reste ici!*' said Pierre in an encouraging tone; and the tired ox was glad, indeed, to stay there."

"But, now, how could the cart go on? How could another ox be put in place of this one? All the other carts were already at the top of the hill. Unlucky Pierre was in despair. What could he do? . . . What could he do?"

François jumped up to stand by his grandfather, and repeated eagerly, "What could he do?--What *did* he do, Grand-père?"

"Listen well," replied his grandfather. "He prayed, my François; and, when he rose from his knees, he saw a strong ox which had come from the trees at the other side of the road. This ox now stood beside the cart as if asking to be allowed to help. With a big gladness in his heart, Pierre fastened him to the cart, and look now--the heavy load, drawn by four oxen as before, was at the top of the hill in front of the great church in no time!"

"Where did the ox come from?" asked François.

"No one knew," answered the old man. "No one ever knew. When Pierre asked the men at the top of the hill if they knew who owned the animal, he was told that no one had ever seen him before. And--what do you think!--even while the men were talking about him as they unloaded this last cart, the stranger ox somehow disappeared! He disappeared, my François, as quickly as he came, and was never seen again. But a boy told Pierre that he saw the ox go back to the woods. 'The ox went right into the woods,' the boy said. The men searched and searched everywhere, but find him they could not."

"And the tired ox?" asked François.

"But yes," said Grand-père Jean, "truly, the tired ox! When Pierre had finished his work he walked down the hill to see him, and--now listen, François--he found that tired ox on his feet, as well and strong as ever!"

"Good!" said François; "there they all are now!" The boy looked up at the towers.

"Those good animals deserve to be there," said his grandfather; "they deserve it--the oxen, and, yes, the horses, too. Patient they were; so willing to help they were! So glad to help and so ready to drag the heavy loads! No wonder they were rewarded by being carved in stone and placed on the towers for everyone to see--century after century! Good beasts! Good beasts!"

As Grand-père Jean ended his story he looked up at the Cathedral towers gleaming in the afternoon light, and nodded his head many times. François, too, kept looking at the towers. Beneath the arcades of the upper portion of the two-storied belfries, the immense figures of the oxen jutted out strong and clear against the blue sky.

"Grand-père," said François, after a minute or two, "tell me--do you know which ox up there is the ox that helped the tired one?"

"No, my François," replied his grandfather; "nobody knows that--no one knows which is the ox that helped."

41

"I do," said François, simply. Then he turned to his marbles and began a new game.

VII. The Raven of the Giralda

ONCE upon a time, a wise raven lived in the top of the Giralda, the Moorish bell tower of the cathedral in Seville, Spain. The raven was old, so old that his head was not black, but gray. The tower, too, is old, and is crowned by the large, bronze figure of Faith which serves as a weather vane. For four centuries, el Girandello, the weather vane, has turned with the wind; and it was four centuries ago, that the raven was living in the tower. All day, he would sit on his perch, with his learned head cocked on one side as he sleepily studied the stonework of the belfry, or alertly discussed weighty matters with his bird comrades and with the wind. At night, he was often deep in talk with his special friend, the owl, who, when tired of roaming through the tops of the giant palm trees or of prowling into out-of-the-way nooks in the cathedral roof, liked to tell of his adventures. For, in night wanderings, the owl sometimes flew near the quiet Guadalquiver which flowed by Seville, and he heard the river murmur tales of the Tower of Gold on its bank; or he peered into the gardens of the Alcazar where Spanish kings had long had their palace, and heard, from the moonbeams, tales which, when repeated, made even the raven's sober thoughts turn sprightly. What the raven liked best to hear was what the owl, or any one else, could tell of the Giralda itself or of the mighty Cathedral below the tower. For the raven cared for nothing in the world so much as he cared for this tall tower, up whose winding passage, of three hundred feet, men had ridden on horseback, almost to the very top. Yes, with his own eyes he had seen those riders. Before the days of the riders, in the time when the bells of the Giralda summoned the Moors to prayer, there had been, on the spire, four large, gilded, copper balls that shone like golden apples. After an earthquake had thrown down the copper balls, el Girandello was placed on the top of the dome. The raven considered himself the owner of el Girandello and, in truth, of all the Giralda. Who, but himself, had perched on the sills of the twin windows that looked out, high in the tower, over the white-roofed Seville? Who, but himself, had stood upon the helmet on the head of el Girandello? Not the owl!--the raven saw to that! And not another bird of his acquaintance, surely! He knew himself to be the oldest raven in the world; he knew himself to be the wisest raven in the world;--and he certainly owned the whole of the Giralda!

The raven, in short, was entirely satisfied with his belfry and its bells. It was a rectangular belfry, and on the four faces of the rectangular stage, high up, were inscribed the four words: *Turris . . . Fortissima . . . Nomen . . . Domini*. The great bells, each christened with holy oil, had their own names. There were Santa Maria and San Juan; there was la Gorda, or The Fat; there was brave San Miguel; there was el Cantor, or The Singer; and there was many another. At times, the bells rang softly through the still air that hovered over the flat-roofed city. At other times, they rang out with such noisy clamor that the vibration penetrated the houses farthest away, and the raven of the Giralda clung to his stone perch as closely as the leaves of the cocoa tree cling to their twigs. The raven liked el Cantor better than all the other bells. He couldn't sing a note himself, but he liked this singing bell, with its especially clear tone. On spring evenings when the fragrance of orange blossoms and acacias filled the air, The Singer would peal forth such a glad note that the people down in the street would say, "El Cantor is feeling fine tonight"; and the raven, up in the tower, would croak loudly with him, though he never croaked with any other bell. Now it happened that the wind, even more than the owl, was a friend of the raven. This was not only because the wind was usually a gentle, lovable, sunny-hearted fellow, but because he was always around the tower, day and night, whereas the owl hid all day. When the raven felt like talking, the wind was always on hand to listen. That was a friend worth having! The wind, too, often told capital stories.

One afternoon, the wind told the raven an astonishing tale. The wind had it from the owl who, in turn, had it from the *passarinno*--that small, gray bird who sings like an angel. To this *passarinno*, the story had come down from his ancestor, of a much earlier time. That ancestor had told it to the wind of his day, who wafted it to the ears of King Alfonso, the Sage. Perhaps, in the later days, it had grown by traveling (*passarinno* to owl, owl to wind, wind to raven); for, when Alfonso, in the thirteenth century, wrote the tale in his big book of *Cantigas*, it wasn't just like the *passarinno's* story to the owl three centuries later. Would you like to hear the tale? Anyone may hear it. To believe the tale as it should be believed, and to understand it aright, you must be able to know the power of melodious sounds, as truly as the blind organist of Seville Cathedral knew that power. If you do not know anything about the music of the trees, or the music of the birds, or the music of the air, you may as well stop reading this story and gather nuts instead. Listen to the tale, if you will; here it is, as the wind told it to the raven.

"For, sir," began the wind," it was a *passarinno* who told the owl and the owl told me. The owl had been praising the voice of the *passarinno*, but the *passarinno* protested and said,

'My voice is nothing compared to the voice of my ancestress—the *passarinna* who entranced the monk.' Now, pray, explain your words,' said the owl. The *passarinno* answered, pleasantly, 'Sit comfortably and I will tell you all.' They were in the garden of the Alcazar and were perched on a tall cocoa tree. The owl settled himself on a wide, sweeping leaf, and the *passarinno* perched himself on a leaf above.

'My ancestress,' the *passarinno* went on, 'was the most marvelous singer ever known. Her home was in the garden, just outside the Court of Oranges beside the Giralda, and when she was singing she would look up at the tower. But she rarely was heard by anyone, because she chose to live in the unfrequented part of the great garden. One morning a monk came, very slowly, along the path that led to the shrubbery where the *passarinna* lived, and my ancestress knew at once three things about that monk: first, that he was good; second, that he was

45

old; third, that he was weary. The monk sat down, rather heavily, beside the fountain that was sending a cool, orange-scented, shimmering spray of water into the air. Leaning over the edge of the pool, he bathed his hands in the clear water and bathed his face. The *passarinna* could plainly see how refreshing, to the tired monk, the water felt; for there came into his face a look like the look on a parched tree when a shower renews it. The weary lines on the monk's brow passed away, as cloud-bars vanish from the evening sky, leaving fairness and tranquillity. He sat, for some time, with a smile on his face, looking up at the tree tops and at the Giralda beyond. Then, kneeling down--and his knees were not as stiff as when he entered the garden--he prayed aloud that he might be permitted to know what the happiness of Paradise would be like. It was at that moment the *passarinna*--marvelous ancestress of mine--began to sing.

'The monk rose from his knees, and, with a smile on his face, seated himself in the thickest part of the shrubbery, where he could see the *passarinna* and where the *passarinna* could see him. That bird of birds sang on and on, now softly, now triumphantly, now wistfully, now ecstatically. There was such charm in her singing, all the leaves forgot to rustle. There was such charm in the melody, the water in the fountain ceased moving--the breezy air was hushed and wondering--the day faded imperceptibly into night, and the stars came nearer earth to hear the song. Still the *passarinna* sang on and on and on. Still the monk listened happily, with an exalted look in his eyes, and was unaware of the passing of hours or of days. As the *passarinna* continued her heavenly song, time itself stopped, though life went on. . . . The monk listened, listened in rapture, while   joyous   satisfaction   held   his   whole being . . . .

'Late one afternoon,' went on the *passarinno*, 'there came to the door of the monastery near the Giralda, an aged, worn-looking man, long-bearded, and in shabby monk's dress. The prior himself answered his knock and said, "Who are you,

46

poor stranger, and what do you want?"

'The monk stammered in much confusion, "Good father, I belong here . . . I left the monastery this morning for a walk. . . . I come back--all is changed. I do not understand. The trees look different . . . the monastery is larger . . . you are not my prior . . . nothing is the same. Where am I? . . . What has happened since morning? . .

I heard a bird sing, and I was so entranced with the song I may have stayed away too long."

'The prior and the brother monks who had now come to the door looked at one another in surprise, and said, in low tones, "He is evidently not himself. . . . The man does not know what he says."

'The prior then spoke to the man, kindly, saying, "What is your name?"

"I am Brother Jubilo," the monk replied; "I mean, . . . he stammered, "that was my name in the monastery . . . that was what I was called this morning."

'The oldest monk among those at the door now looked thoughtful. It was to him that the others always turned whenever any knowledge of the past was wanted. "Attend my words," he suddenly said to the prior. "Three hundred years ago a brother monk, named Jubilo, wandered off and was never again seen. My Father--my brother monks—I am of the opinion that we have before us, this day, a true marvel! I am sure this poor monk and that Jubilo, of three hundred years ago, are the same!"

'Then the prior, believing, took the monk warmly by the hand and brought him into the monastery, and all rejoiced.'

'That, 'said the *passarinno* to the owl, 'is the story of my ancestress, the *passarinna* of long ago. The Giralda knows I speak truth.'

And the wind, as he finished the tale, remarked, "That's all the story, sir; but the *passarinno* does speak truth."

47

"Truth it is," replied the raven, "and I'll keep the story going."

Then the sunny wind brushed the tail feathers of the raven and blew along his leisurely way, through the streets of Seville.

The raven sat stolidly in his niche, gazing with keen eyes at the city spread out below the Giralda--its flat-roofed houses gleaming in soft colors, from blue and gray to palest pink. He watched the women watering their carnations on the roofs. He saw the motionless, dusky Guadalquiver, in the late afternoon light. His eyes followed the group of boys coming to the Cathedral to practice their solemn dance. Turning his wise, old head, he looked toward the gardens of the Alcazar, then down at the Court of Oranges, and at the roof of the vast Cathedral below him--its parapets, and buttresses. His roving gaze went all over the city until sundown. The bells of the Giralda sent out their evening peal, and el Cantor's vibrating tone fell softly on the waiting breeze. The raven sturdily croaked, croaked, until el Cantor stopped singing; then, humping himself into a ball, he tucked his head under his feathers and went to sleep.

VIII. The Goblin of Giotto's Tower

NO ONE has ever seen the goblin of Giotto's Tower, though many have heard its voice and any flower vender, in the busy square in Florence where the tower stands, can tell you the legend of the little goblin. This lively sprite is the real guardian of Giotto's Campanile, or Shepherd's Tower. When one mounts the stairs of the tower, a gentle voice is heard below, saying:

"Go   on,   go   on,   Signora,
Go   up   the   stairs,--oh,   go!
Be   not   afraid,   my   Lady,
For I am here below."

Some people think this encouraging word comes from the guide or from a fellow-sightseer. For it's oddly true that fully half the grown-ups in the world and one-sixth of the children never see goblins or fairies even when the little beings are cutting capers directly in front of their noses. Yet, in Florence, there is many a "folletto" or protecting spirit, fairy or goblin, who gives special favor to anything worth while. Now every one knows that Giotto's Tower is decidedly worth while, for it is one of the most beautiful towers ever built. So, of course, it has its own "folletto," for all time. On moon-lit nights, you can often see the shadow of the "folletto," if you look at the left of the center bas-relief, on the west side of the tower--the bas-relief that shows the herdsman, Jabal, sitting in his tent and looking out at his sheep and a lamb. A wise, little puppy is sitting at the right, outside the tent, with his careful eyes on the sheep. But, just as you come near the shadow of the goblin, (for you are sure it is the actual shadow) to--it is gone!

A few miles northeast of Florence, the town of Fiesole perches on a high hill, and a few miles beyond Fiesole, is the small town of Vespignano, nestling high up in the Apennines. Six centuries ago, the rolling fields and green trees of Vespignano looked much as they do today, and the ilex, the 'oak and the olive gave a welcome shade to the herdsman. Beneath a wide-spreading oak tree, one sunny, spring day, in the year 1286, a ten-year-old boy lay on the grass, his chin resting in his hands. His father's sheep were grazing all over the field. Giotto's eyes were not on the sheep this moment, but on the gnarled, gray-green olive trees, far off on the hills. There was always so much for Giotto di Bondone to see, while he was tending the sheep, that the hours of the long day flew like the wind, and, if his little dog hadn't been always on the alert for straying lambs, who knows what might sometimes have happened? But the good dog, hardly more than a puppy, was occupied, hour after hour, with his serious work of watching the sheep, so that the boy, ever on the look-out for the things of interest in the near field or on the distant hills, could let his thoughts roam, free as a bird, wherever they liked.

Giotto was a boy who loved to draw, and he was constantly looking, looking at the things around him with the thought of putting them on his slate. He kept by him a piece of slate on which he would draw, with a pointed stone, whatever attracted his eye. Even when he wasn't drawing, he liked to look at a tree, a goat, or anything whatever, and think how he might draw it so that it would look just as solid on his slate as it looked in the field. Sometimes he would laughingly watch his little dog barking excitedly at a straying sheep; sometimes he would gaze absorbedly at one of the sheep standing still, or at the thick neck of a donkey in a neighboring field; or, with half-shut eyes, he would dreamily follow the motions of some boys climbing into the great oak which stood farther up on the hillside. He never tired of watching the way the wind turned back the oak leaves and lifted them in masses that emphasized the solid structure of the tree. The birds, too, that at times, came very near him, especially pleased him; for they had a habit of standing in attentive little groups, as if, he said to himself, they were waiting for some one to talk to them. For several minutes, he would silently watch them, until, at last, his chuckling laugh would send them flying away.

Yet Giotto's father remarked to a neighbor, "A fine boy to work is that boy of mine! . . . He's almost old enough to apprentice to the wool merchant."

There had been in the flock of sheep, until three days ago, one little lamb so fond of Giotto that it would never roam around the field with the other lambs and sheep, but would stay, all day, close to the boy's side. Under the oak tree where Giotto was now lying, was a large, flat stone on which the lamb used to lie. In fact, the lamb had liked so much to lie there that Giotto had named the stone The Lamb's Stone. Giotto had told one of his boy friends that this lamb truly talked to him. "*Da vero*," declared Giotto, with a twinkling smile, "the lamb often asks me to lie down with it on this big stone." So, to please the lamb, Giotto would sometimes put his head down on the stone. Three mornings ago, the little lamb, at first full of frisky gambols as usual, became quiet and somehow not like itself. By afternoon, it had become unable to stand, and suddenly, to Giotto's dismay, appeared too weak to live. Just as Giotto realized this, the lamb had raised its head from the stone where it lay, and said:

"Giotto, be not astonished
That I thus speak to thee;
I have such love for thee,
Wherever thou shalt go,
I will follow thee always
In the form of a fairy;
And through my favour
Thou shalt become a great sculptor
And artist."

Then the lamb had died.

Today, Giotto, dreaming deep day dreams under the oak tree, saw everything near and far, especially the near. A herdsman, going down the slope, took his attention, for, to Giotto, the figure of the man looked thick and solid, surprisingly solid, outlined against the field. The sheep,

51

cropping the grass, seemed continually to give new turns to their placid heads. The boy liked to look at the actual form of anything. His rambling thought now went back to his little lamb on that morning when it had been frolicsome and had stood with a funny, thoughtful turn of its head before it took droll, capering steps. Presently Giotto took up his slate and began to draw, saying aloud, "*Agnello mio*, I'm going to draw you exactly as you looked." Gradually, there appeared on the slate the form of the spirited little lamb. So intent was the boy on his drawing that he didn't notice a man who had been watching the growing picture of the lamb. When Giotto finally looked up a moment from his drawing, he was astonished to see, standing near him, a man in the dress of a noble.

"Boy," said the man, "I see you like to draw."

Giotto gave a quick glance straight at the face of the man, and smiled.

"That lamb must be your own lamb; it's so natural it looks alive," added the man.

A twinkle came into Giotto's eye. Yet he felt, at once, stirred within himself. Who could this great man be who cared to stop beside a mere boy to look at his drawing? Something about him drew Giotto strongly.

"My boy," said the noble, "have you a father?"

"*Si, Signore*," replied Giotto, wonderingly.

"When you go home," continued the man, "ask your father if he will let you go to Florence to study drawing under me. I should like to have you in my workshop. My name is Cimabue."

Then the boy rose quickly, and with a flush in his face, said, stammeringly, "I will, *Signore* . . . I will ask him to-day." For Giotto had, of course, heard of the great artist, Cimabue-- the greatest painter of the time--and could hardly believe his own good fortune.

"You would like to study drawing?" went on Cimabue.

"*Si, Signore,*" said Giotto, with all his heart in his voice. Like to study drawing? . . . Like to study under the great Cimabue? . . . Wasn't drawing the one thing in life he wanted to do? . . . Something within him shouted for joy!

Then Cimabue, looking down again at the drawing on the slate, put his hand on the boy's shoulder and said, somewhat gravely, "You have taught me something, *mi' figlio,* and it may be that I can teach you something." With a pleasant nod, he walked on, leaving the young Giotto in a whirl of new ideas.

The noble seemed to the boy the most wonderful person he had ever seen. No one before had ever noticed his drawing. No one had ever told him that it was worth while for him to draw. He drew because he felt he must. How kind a voice the man had! How he had looked and looked at this simple little lamb! Giotto had now a keen desire to see the paintings which Cimabue had done; for a man like that would surely paint glorious pictures. The thought of going to Florence to study drawing under him rushed through his whole being, as a mighty wind rushes through the trees. Something within him was suddenly freed. He felt lifted up and tingling with joyful expectation; all because of a compelling power in the noble, a power which the boy could not explain. He felt as though he himself, some day, would do great things--he, only Giotto di Bondone, watching his father's sheep!

Years passed. The wool merchant lost "a fine boy for work," but the world gained a great artist. Giotto painted at Assisi, Padua, and Florence, frescoes of such power and freedom that all who saw them realized that here was an entirely new way of expressing life. For the man Giotto looked at men with the same understanding eyes with which the young Giotto had watched the sheep and the oak trees on the hillside; and he painted his human figures in firm reality as he had dreamed of doing. As a boy, he had looked with his own eyes; as a man, he still looked with his own eyes; and, because he so looked,

53

painting, in his hands, became a new thing.

When the Cathedral in Florence was built, Giotto designed and commenced the Campanile, the beautiful bell tower. Some of the bas-reliefs are his own work; some are by his friend and pupil, Andrea Pisano; and some, which are by other sculptors, are carved from Giotto's designs. The bas-relief of Jabal--whoever made it--has, in it, a thought of the small hill-town of Vespignano and the brown-skinned boy with his sheep.

When you stand near the Shepherd's Tower--Giotto's Tower--in the midst of the fruit and flower venders, you will see, from pavement to cornice, exquisite paneling of white marble, red porphyry, and green serpentine that is like the soft green of Giotto's field. You will see finely wrought capitals of the windows, lace-like design, and beauty, everywhere. If you belong to the portion of the world that never sees goblins, you will not see even the shadow of the goblin of the tower. If you belong to the fortunate portion that sees and hears all that there is to see and hear, you will easily believe the tale of Lucia, the flower vender, when she points to the bas-relief of the little lamb outside Jabal's tent and says: "The folletto of this tower is Giotto's lamb, you understand; yes, the lamb's spirit it is that guards so well our beautiful tower."

When you mount the stairs you will hear a voice saying encouragingly:

"Go   on,   go   on,   Signora,
Go   up   the   stairs,--oh,   go!
Be   not   afraid,   my   Lady,
For I am here below."

As you hear the voice, you will have a momentary glimpse of a boy on a far-away hillside playing with his little lamb, and you will know that you really hear the voice of the spirit of the lamb--the guardian spirit of Giotto's Tower.

IX. The Leprechaun of Ardmore Tower

THE Leprechaun--that flash from elf-land--was perched comfortably upon the west window ledge, high up in Ardmore Tower. Dawn was just beginning to send misty, gray lights over the rolling land. Winds that have blown since the world began were blowing around the old Irish tower. It was the south wind, this morning, that was blowing the strongest--the wind from the good sea that washed the coast of Ardmore and the high-lands of Ireland. The strong, stone tower, tapering skyward, stood, as it stands today, like a silent sentinel on the "hill of the sheep"-- the "great hill." Below its conical top, two windows, east and west, looked out, and it's on the ledge of the west one--mind you--that the Leprechaun was sitting. He had been sitting there since sundown. An iron bar, inside the tower, goes from the top of the west window to the top of the east window, and once, no one knows how long ago, seven small bells hung from this bar under the pinnacle. They are gone now, but in the old days they used to ring often.

("That's so," said the Leprechaun. He was always saying "That's so," to agree with himself or other people--himself oftenest.)

This little elf, in red jacket and green breeches who spends most of his days and some of his nights making shoes for the fairy folk, has been working the past night on a pair of riding boots for the fairy prince who wants the boots by sunrise. Tap, tap, tap--goes the Leprechaun's tiny hammer. Whish, whish, go his swift fingers. Hum, hum-m-m-m-, goes his little singing tune, for the Leprechaun could no more work without singing than you could sleep without shutting your eyes.

("That's so!" said the Leprechaun.)

He is only six inches high, and harder to catch than a will-o'-the-wisp. If one *could* ever succeed in catching him, and then could keep looking at him, he *might* tell--though not a bit willingly--where a wonderful crock of gold is. But do you think you could keep looking at him and at him alone? Why, just as you think you are looking at nothing else, he, somehow, makes you look away from him, and, ochone, he is gone! He's that clever.

("That's so," said the Leprechaun.)

Many an enchantment the Leprechaun can perform, for all he appears so simple as he pegs away at the riding boots. Yes, himself it is that can blight the corn or snip off hair most unexpectedly. When he sits, crosslegged at his work, whether on a cornice of a roof or on a twig of the low bushes, it's just as well not to let him know you are watching him. The Irish fairy folk are all like that, and draw magic out of earth and sea and sky, or else draw it out of nothing at all.

("Do you hear that?" said the Leprechaun.)

Now this misty, windy dawn of a morning, thousands of days and nights ago, as the Leprechaun, up there on the gray, stone tower, tapped, tapped with his hammer, to finish the prince's boots, promised by sunrise, his elfin mind capered around with many thoughts. The mists were beginning to shine in the dim light of early morning, and the Leprechaun's thoughts, freshened by the south wind, were wafted over the whole land of Erin that stretched beyond the bogs and swamps, beyond the mounds and cromlechs, beyond the hills. He could tell you the colors of all the winds of Ireland. This south wind was white; the north wind, full of blackness; the west wind pale yellow; and the east wind was always a stirring, purple wind. The lesser winds, too, had their colors--yellow of furze, red of fire, gray of fog, green of meadow, brown of autumn leaves, and three more colors that mortals could not see. The Leprechaun, whenever he wished, could travel lightly on whatever wind was blowing and sing a tune as loud as any of them. This morning, in the misty dawn, it was his heart that did the traveling and it was his thoughts that sang tunes to match. When his eyes glanced from his work, toward the sea, his thoughts flew to

Manannan Mac Lir, the old sea-god, riding along in his chariot, with thousands of his steeds shaking their manes as they galloped with him. For many a century, the great, slender, round tower had watched these steeds and the spirited charioteer. On many a moonlit night, it had seen invading bands crawl quietly to shore and stealthily march right up to the base of the tower with bad plans to surprise the unprotected people. Again and again the men of Ardmore had gathered their families, with provisions, safely, into the tall tower, barring the narrow door that was many feet high above the ground. There the weak ones and the women and children had lived, for days, until the invaders had been driven away. The Leprechaun laughed aloud as he thought of one stormy day when the old sea-god, Manannan Mac Lir, had bidden his horses keep the invaders from reaching the shore and the tower. The lively horses shook their manes and obeyed--ochone, but they obeyed!

Tap, tap, tap! The south wind, thought the Leprechaun, will be a strong one, this day! And the wind will draw music from the harps of all the Little Good Folk throughout Erin. As the Leprechaun, between his taps, looked westward, there was a break in the light morning vapor, like the gay snatch of song a maiden sings in the midst of her work; and, through the break, the elf's long gaze swept across the river Blackwater, and beside Watergrasshill, over the moor-land to the Bochragh Mountains, and even as far as Mt. Mish. There was a tale about Mt. Mish that rushed in now upon his thinking--a tale about his ancestors, the Tuatha-de-Danann "the folk of the god whose mother is Dana."

On a day, in the early age of the world, when gray moor-land and steep mountains began to blaze brilliant with purple heather and yellow furze, the Danaans, covering themselves with a fog, crept along the east coast to possess the country near Mt. Mish. Fiercely they fought with the inhabitants, the Firbolgs, and won. For a thousand years they held sway--these tall, fair-haired men of Greek descent who had come from the North. After the thousand years and one day more, new invaders, the Milesians, entering along the bank of the Inverskena River, swept up into the land, like the knowing conquerors that they were, to overcome the Danaans.

The Leprechaun now sang, with a little humming chant, the words that Amergin, chief druid of the Milesians, sang when he set his right foot on the soil of Erin:

	I	am	the	Wind	that	blows	over	the	sea,
I		am	the	Wave		of	the		ocean;
I		am	the	Murmur		of	the		billows;
I		am	the	Ox	of	the	seven		combats;
I		am	the	Vulture		upon	the		rock;
I		am	a	Ray		of	the		Sun;
I		am	the		fairest		of		Plants;

. . . .

When the Danaans had been conquered by the Milesians, they promised that they would dwell inside the hills or under the lakes, and that they would be invisible to mortals, except on rare occasions. This promise they had kept.

("That's so," said the Leprechaun.)

The Leprechaun liked what the Danaans, his ancestors, had done next. The chief druid of the Danaans had raised his golden harp in the dazzling sunlight, the other druids had lifted their silver harps in the glittering morning air, and all the druids had played such deliciously enchanting melodies that the Danaans, in a long procession that seemed like a living green, had followed their leaders, laughing as they went, and singing like merry brooks or happy children. Into the mountains they had gone, disappearing before the very eyes of the Milesians. Forever afterwards they lived within the mountains and became the Ever-Living Living Ones in the Land of Youth.

The Leprechaun knew well that he, and all his elf kin, were descendants of those very Danaans, who still lived in their underground palaces that blazed with light and laughter. Hadn't the *drean*--the wise, small wren--that druid of birds, often told him what was going on down there? Hadn't he himself been below the tower of Ardmore, where, in a glorious hall that belonged to the Ever-Living Living Ones, the Danaans held many a gay carousal? Didn't he hear, at times, their bells ringing under the bog, on a quiet evening? And hadn't he, more times than once, rung the sweet bells of Ardmore--these bells which never had been rung except by one whose real home was in the Land of Youth? In the Land of Youth was the Leprechaun's home. (Ochone, I should say!) There it had been since the day that Oisin, son of Finn, journeyed to that land. For, on the same day, without Oisin's knowledge, the Leprechaun had sped from the green hills of Erin, through a golden haze, to the country of the Ever-Living Living Ones. Oisin was his hero, his great hero, whom he had helped, invisibly, more than he had helped anyone else. The most valiant Danaan of all was Oisin, and Oisin he would follow to the world's end. ("That's so," said the Leprechaun, as he began the fancy stitching on the prince's riding boots.)

Now, for the thousandth time, he told himself the story of Oisin, for he liked this tale best of all: how Oisin, when hunting, met the maiden, Niam of the Golden Hair, riding her snow-white steed; how, after she sang to him a song of the enchanting "land beyond dreams," Oisin had ridden with her to the Land of Youth (and the Leprechaun, in the shape of a butterfly, had perched on the horse's mane); how, in the realm of her father, the king, fearless Oisin had had brave adventures. He rescued a princess from a giant; subdued the three Hounds of Erin (helped by the Leprechaun who confused the hounds), and found the magic harp--a harp next in wonder to the Dagda's harp whose strings, when touched, would sing the story of the one who last touched them. He had even tilted with the king's cupbearer to win a gold-hilted sword, and had done other worthy deeds. No time at all, it seemed to Oisin, that magical time, in the Land of Youth, but, at last, his heart longed to see his old home. So Niam of the Golden Hair gave him her snow-white steed to ride, but charged him three times that, when he should reach the familiar places of Erin, he must not, once, set foot upon the ground or he would never be able to return to the Land of Youth. Oisin bade her farewell and, with the Leprechaun as a butterfly still on the horse's mane, he began his homeward journey.

As he was riding along, once more, through a beautiful vale of Erin, he saw men, much smaller than himself, trying in vain to push aside a huge boulder that had rolled from the hillside down upon their tilled land. In pity for these weaklings, he instantly jumped from his saddle to the ground (not heeding the Leprechaun who, in his own form, clung with all his might, to remind him of Niam's warning) and, with one push, he sent the boulder out of the way. Alas! Even as the men were shouting praises to their god-like helper, it seemed to Oisin that darkness bore him to the earth. When he opened his eyes, lo, he was an old man, feeble, gray-headed, gray-bearded! The men whom he had helped, had with one accord run away; but the Leprechaun, astride a twig close by, whispered words of cheer and sang part of the song of the Danaans when they went into the mountains. Oisin then roused himself and said faintly, "I hear the voice of bells." Then he added in a resolute tone, "Whenever I shall hear sweet bells ring, young will be my heart." Since that day, the Leprechaun had often rung bells, especially the bells of Ardmore Tower, because he knew that Oisin would hear them and feel young again.

Tap, tap, tap,--and the Leprechaun's work is done. It's little that anyone can tell about him making shoes, or about Ireland's heroes, or about its grassy mounds of mystery. He stands up now and stretches himself. If he felt like it, he could blow a blast on the tiny, curved horn, hanging at his side, and call, from the Underland, as many merry-hearted Danaans as he chose. He could cast spells, too, on the sea, beyond the ninth wave from shore. Instead, he whisks from the west window into the tower and out again, through the east window. There he stands for a few moments--his feet braced on the highest circular cornice, his back leaning against the sloping roof top-- watching the rim of the sun rise over a mountainous cloud. The sky of gold is changing to the pink of a wild rose. The gray mists, over moorland and mound, are scattering as quickly as the men whom Oisin helped.

The Round Tower of Ardmore again greeted the sun, as the Leprechaun, hugging tightly the riding boots promised to the fairy prince at sunrise, swiftly slid down a sunbeam to the top of the oak tree, where the prince was waiting.

"Here they are, Your Highness," said the elf, with a bow.

The prince smiled, as he took the boots, and gave the Leprechaun a piece of gold. "You've kept your promise," he said.

"That's so," answered the Leprechaun. Then he sprang up on the rollicking south wind and flew away.

X. The Tower That Sings

THE golden plover, perched on a low bush near the old Pawnee Indian, Lone-Chief, began talking. Lone-Chief was looking across the Cimarron, a river of Oklahoma, near which the Pawnee tribe had been allowed, by the white men, to live. Lone-Chief looked across the river, puffed at his long pipe and listened. Lone-Chief listened.

"I have heard of it since I was last here, two hundred sunrises ago," said the golden plover. "During my flight to the North, it has happened. I have heard of a tower that sings."

The golden plover pruned his feathers, waiting for Lone-Chief to speak.

Lone-Chief puffed calmly at his pipe, but said nothing.

"There is a tower that sings," repeated the golden plover. "A tower there is that sings like all the birds."

Again the plover waited.

Lone-Chief, almost as motionless as the ground on which he was sitting, said nothing.

"The tower is in the land of flowers," went on the golden plover, "in the land of sunshine--the land of birds. The tower sings each day, at sunset. This is a true thing. It was told to me by my brother, the golden plover of Lake-of-the-Hills. The tower is on an iron mountain. The tower is of stone, and sings."

Lone-Chief puffed several minutes, in silence, then slowly took the pipe from his mouth. "My son," he said, in a calm tone, "the tower does not sing. The stone tower never sings. Hearken to me. In the beginning, Tirawa, the Great Spirit, appointed the stations of the stars. He bade Bright Star--the evening star, the Mother of all things--stand in the West. He bade Great Star, the morning star, stand in the East. He bade Star-That-Does-Not-Move--star-chief of the skies--stand in the

North. He bade Spirit Star stand in the South, but to be seen, by men, only at a certain time in the year. He bade all the stars sing. He bade the stars sing at morn.

"Hearken to me, my son. There are things on earth that also sing. Hearken to my words, for I am one who has seen hundreds of moons. I am one to whom has come down, from my grandfather, knowledge of our tribe, knowledge of other tribes, knowledge of the earth on which all dwell. Ages ago, the people on the earth were many; so many that, if a count could be made of all the stars in the sky, all the feathers on birds, all the hairs and furs on animals, all the hairs of men's heads, the first people would be even more in number. Now, in that long-ago time, a tribe came, in its wanderings toward the sunrise, to a muddy river. They camped there. They rested there. The next day they came to another river. Two winters, two harvests, they lived there. They went, then, to the end of the river and heard a noise as of thunder. They went nearer to find whence the noise came. They found a red smoke and, beyond the smoke, a mountain. The mountain thundered, and on the mountain was a sound as of singing. The singing noise came from the great fire that blazed upward. Later, they found a red and yellow fire that came to them out of the North. This fire they mingled with fire from the mountain. This fire is used today and this, too, sometimes sings. Also, they found four herbs which sang, and, to this day, we use these singing herbs for healing.

"Hearken again, my son. For there are other things that sing. When the rain-god dips his great brush, made of feathers of the birds of the heavens, into the lakes of the skies and sprinkles the cornfields with refreshing rain, the rain-drops sing for gladness. When Tirawa sends his breath through the tree tops, the trees sing all the day or all the night. Once, too, when no winds blew, an elderberry tree, far to the west from here, made music. It sang a song of its own, both by day and by night. And Wek-wek it was who found the song-tree and took a piece of it home and planted it. Then other elderberry song-trees grew.

"Hearken further, my son. When I, a boy, fasted and made my tribal prayer (the clay on my head, my bow and arrow in my hand), the vision that came to me was a bird--the song of Tonatzuli, sacred sun-bird. Thousands of paces have I gone since then, and Tonatzuli, heavenly singer, has always been ready to give me aid. All birds of earth that sing have, each, one note of Tonatzuli's song.

"Now this I tell you, my son. The brooks sing, the rivers sing, the summer breezes sing, the storm winds sing, children's voices and old men's voices sing. But stone sings not. The tower of stone sings not. The tower on the mountain of iron sings not."

Lone-Chief put his pipe into his mouth and smoked in silence, looking calmly at the golden plover. For a few moments longer, the plover remained on the bush. Then, with his clear "too-lee-lee lee-lu-wit," he flew down to the ground beside Lone-Chief.

"My father," began the golden plover, "I fly each year from farthest South to farthest North. I fly each year from farthest North to farthest South. When Winter-maker comes with his cold winds, fierce snows and frozen waters, southward I fly. When the first thunder in the spring warns us that winter is at an end and the time of planting is drawing near, northward I fly. I see the sky touching earth on every side. I see prairies, rivers, forests, mountains, oceans. All the birds I know. Ki-ki-ah, the mountain blue jay who plants acorns so freely that oak trees abound--Ki-ki-ah is my friend. Olelle, that bird of my own shape, who lives in a cold spring deep down underneath the water, I sometimes see when he comes up in early morning and flies away. Wak-ko-lot-ko, the great, blue heron, I have talked with many a day. Beautiful Sialia, the bluebird, whose voice flows in joy, has taken short flights beside me. I have flown near the ancient-seeming pelican. I have followed O-shi-hi-yi, the mocking bird. I have watched the eagle, the All-flier, soaring along the path of the rainbow to the mountain-height. I have listened to the words of the dove. Only one bird I have not seen--the giant cloud-bird, that Bird of Ages, the clapping of whose wings is the thunder, the glancing of whose eye is the lightning--from whose white breast the snow of winter falls; but all other birds I know."

The golden plover paused a moment.

"My father," he added, "under the corn moon tonight I go on with my southward flight. I have rested here to tell you of the tower that sings like all the birds."

"Go, my son," then said Lone-Chief, slowly; "go--and bring me word again. While you have been speaking, Tonatzuli, heavenly bird, bird of my vision, has told me I am to believe your report, whatever it may be. The pledge of bird is sacred. Bird can do more than man. Bird can float in the air and on the wind. Bird can soar toward heaven and the gods. Bird can fly over high mountains, when man must walk. Bird can dart like the lightning and travel like the sun. Bird can spurn the clouds-- can make wind by the spreading of his wings. His plumage is of the sunset--his song the earliest music of the world. Go, my son; fly over goldenrod, fly over the golden corn and above the autumn trees of gold, until you reach the land of flowers and the tower of stone on the mountain of iron. But when the first corn is planted, return to me. Return at the time of the first planting."

The golden plover flew to the branch of a thick oak tree, where he perched for a few minutes, his spangled, golden and black feathers shimmering in the September sun. Soft trills rippled from his throat; then came a burst of melodious song

"chee-lee-u-too-lee-ee,
tee-lee-lee, tu-lee-lu-wit"

and he was aloft in the air and away. The Pawnee Indian, smoking his long pipe, stared after the bird, as the golden plover flew along, now rising, now dipping, and, at last, drifted out of sight in the hazy southeast.

Beside Mountain Lake, in the Florida highlands, there

65

stands a tower that has caught, in marble and stone, the flush of the dawn. The tower rises from the top of Iron Mountain, midway between the blue Gulf of Mexico and the Atlantic Ocean, a mountain held sacred by the Indians of old. Here, they reverenced the sun. Here, they performed their solemn Corn Dance. The region that encircles the tower is thronged by trees-- the palm, the pine, the laurel, magnolias, and live oaks. Here and there, amidst the green of the trees, gleam, in radiant color, lilies, orchids, wild plum, iris, dogwood, and acacia. Flaming azalias greet the sun. Fragrant jasmine sweetens the air. Bird notes sound everywhere. The pinnacles of the tower are adorned with representations of the crane, the pelican and the flamingo; and on the upper balconies are carved great eagles, with folded wings, and doves, carrying laurel and oak, in token of peace.

It was to this tower that the golden plover came, one evening, near the time of sunset. Among the many birds near him, on the tall, live oak on which he lit, was a chestnut-sided warbler.

"I am a stranger here," the golden plover said at once to the warbler. "I have a nesting-place, farther south, to which I have always gone by a different course. But, this autumn, I have flown out of my way to learn about this tower. My brother says it sings. Have you ever heard it sing?"

"It sings every day," said the warbler; "and sings like all the fairest winds that blow."

Then the golden plover turned to a mocking bird, above him, and asked, "Have you, too, heard the tower sing?"

"I live here all the time to hear its song," answered the mocking bird. "It sings like rippling lakes."

"And you, thrush?" inquired the golden plover. "Do you tell me the tower sings?"

"The tower sings as wondrously as the nightingale," replied the thrush.

66

"The nightingale?" said the golden plover, in surprised tone. "I do not know that bird."

"You will hear him in a moment," said the thrush, "for he always starts for us the evening song." And as the delicate pink of the tower, reflected in the lake below, became more glowing in the sunset light, a deep, rich trill, even then, began, followed by a song that seemed to float down from heaven itself. All the birds, on shrub or tree or lake border, listened to the glorious song. The white ibis uttered once his "crook, croo, croo," and then was still. Stately, scarlet flamingoes perched on one leg and made no sound. The quail, the towhee, the pink curlew, the roseate spoon-bill, the cardinal, the little, laughing wren, and every bird, large or small, forgot his own song while listening to the nightingale's. Finally, the mocking bird took up some of the notes of the nightingale's song, and then all the birds who could sing, or chirp, or whistle, joined in a great chorus of joy.

When the singing ceased, a strange thing happened in the golden plover's hearing. The air was filled, all at once, with liquid, bell-like notes that seemed to come from the tower itself--that pink-hued tower of marble and stone. Not a bird was singing, no water was rippling, no tree rustled. Yet a harmony of sound, that thrilled the whole being of the golden plover, sprang earthward, upward, outward, skyward. To the plover, it was as if earth and all its people, the sky and all its clouds and stars, had burst into one melodious, inimitable song--a song such as Tonatzuli--heard only in dreams--might sing.

Winter-maker had gone to the Arctic region, and the first thunder of spring murmured in the south-land. The golden plover, winging swiftly in a northwesterly direction, came, in a straight line, to the Cimarron River. On a mild morning in early March, he greeted Lone-Chief who was sitting in front of his wigwam.

"Tee-lee-lee tu-lee-lu-wit," sang the bird. "My father, I have heard the tower that sings. It sings like all the birds of the world and like something beyond the birds."

Lone-Chief sat immovable. He sat as if unheeding. Many minutes passed. At length, the stolid Indian spoke.

"My son," he began, "there comes to me, now, a fragment of a mountain song made by a tribe not our own. My grand-father heard it from a Navajo Indian who fell into his hands. My grandfather sang it to me when I was young. This is the song."

Then the aged Indian chanted aloud, on the morning breeze:

```
    (Thither                      go                    I!)
Chief            of              all                nations
(Thither                    go                       I!)
Living                                              forever
(Thither go I!)

    Blessings                                     bestowing
(Thither                    go                       I!)
Calling         me,       "Son,        my            son!"
(Thither go I!)
```

"Golden plover," said Lone-Chief, to the bird whose fear-less eyes looked into his own, "Tonatzuli tells me your words speak truth. Were I a youth, I would start before yonder cloud moves a finger's breadth--I would start this moment to the land of flowers to hear the tower that sings."

www.ingramcontent.com/pod-product-compliance
Lightning Source LLC
Chambersburg PA
CBHW060216290526
45789CB00003B/1290